Kate and Tuck

by Myka-Lynne Sokoloff
illustrated by Sophie Hanton

It was a cool fall day.

"Wear a sweater," Kate's mom said.

Kate got a sweater for Tuck, too.
"You look great," she told Tuck.

Mack was raking leaves.
"Come jump!" he said.

Kate and Tuck went outside.
It was a cold winter day.

Kate's mom said, "Wear
mittens, boots, and a scarf."

Kate gave Tuck a scarf, too.

Mack was playing in
the snow.
"Watch out!" he yelled.

Kate and Tuck went out in the warm spring rain.

Kate's mom said, "Wear boots and a raincoat."

Kate said, "Tuck has boots, too. Doesn't she look great?"

A truck went by.
Bad luck!

It was a hot summer day.

"Wear a hat and sunglasses,"
Kate's mom said.

Kate gave Tuck glasses, too.
"We look great, Tuck,"
she said.